The Coast Path follows the gentle shores of the West Fleet lagoon (Stage 41)

SOUTH WEST COAST PATH
VOLUME 3: PLYMOUTH TO POOLE

This guidebook describes part of the southern section of the 630-mile (1015km) South West Coast Path National Trail. It covers the trail from Plymouth to Poole along the Devon and Dorset coastline. This convenient and compact booklet of Ordnance Survey 1:25,000 maps shows the route, providing all of the mapping you need to walk the trail in either direction.

Contents and using this guide
This booklet of Ordnance Survey 1:25,000 Explorer maps has been designed for convenient use on the trail and includes:
- a key to map pages (page 4–5) showing where to find the maps for each stage.
- the full and up-to-date line of the National Trail
- an extract from the OS Explorer map legend (pages 105–107).

In addition, the *South West Coast Path* guidebook describes the full route from end to end alongside all you need to know to plan a successful trip and lots of incidental information about local history, geography and wildlife.

© Cicerone Press 2023
Second edition 2023
ISBN-13: 978 1 78631 200 6
First edition 2017
Photos © Paddy Dillon 2017

© Crown copyright and database rights
OS PU100012932

SOUTH WEST COAST PATH SOUTH

Stages 1–17 . . . . Volume 1: Minehead to St Ives
Stages 18–30 . . . . Volume 2: St Ives to Plymouth

Stage 31	Plymouth to Wembury Beach	6
Stage 32	Wembury Beach to Bigbury-on-Sea	9
Stage 33	Bigbury-on-Sea to Salcombe	15
Stage 34	Salcombe to Stoke Fleming	19
Stage 35	Stoke Fleming to Brixham	26
Stage 36	Brixham to Shaldon	31
Stage 37	Shaldon to Budleigh Salterton	36
Stage 38	Budleigh Salterton to Seaton	43
Stage 39	Seaton to Seatown	52
Stage 40	Seatown to Abbotsbury	59
Stage 41	Abbotsbury to Ferrybridge	65
Stage 42	Isle of Portland circuit	69
Stage 43	Ferrybridge to Lulworth Cove	75
Stage 44	Lulworth Cove to Swanage	81
Stage 45	Swanage to South Haven Point	93

SOUTH DORSET RIDGEWAY
West Bexington to Osmington Mills 97

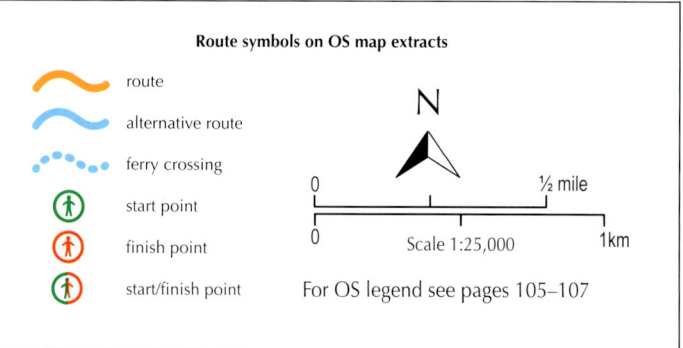

A Coast Path walker trudges up to a marker post above Ivy Cove

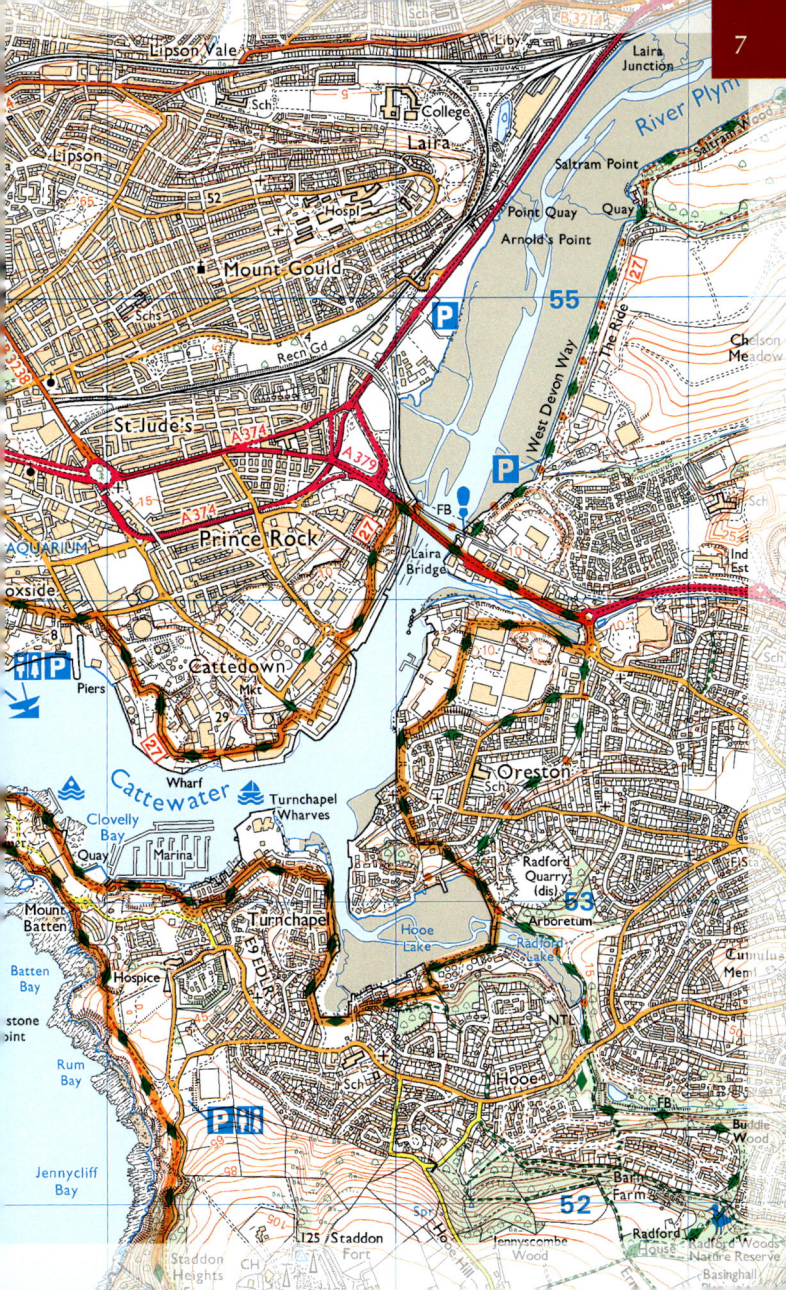

12

Bigbury-on-Sea to Wembury Beach
Start   Car park, Bigbury-on-Sea
Finish   Marine Centre, Wembury
Distance   25km (15½ miles)
Time   8hr

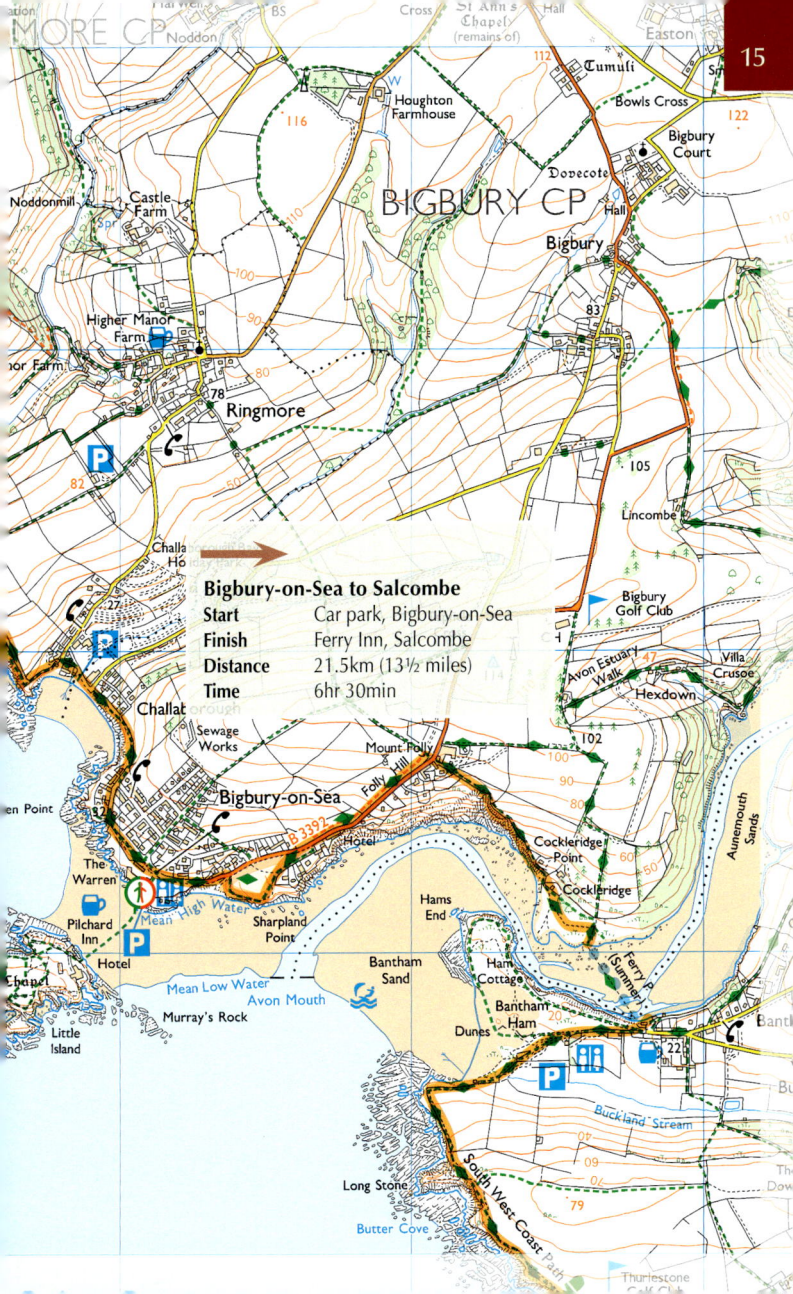

16

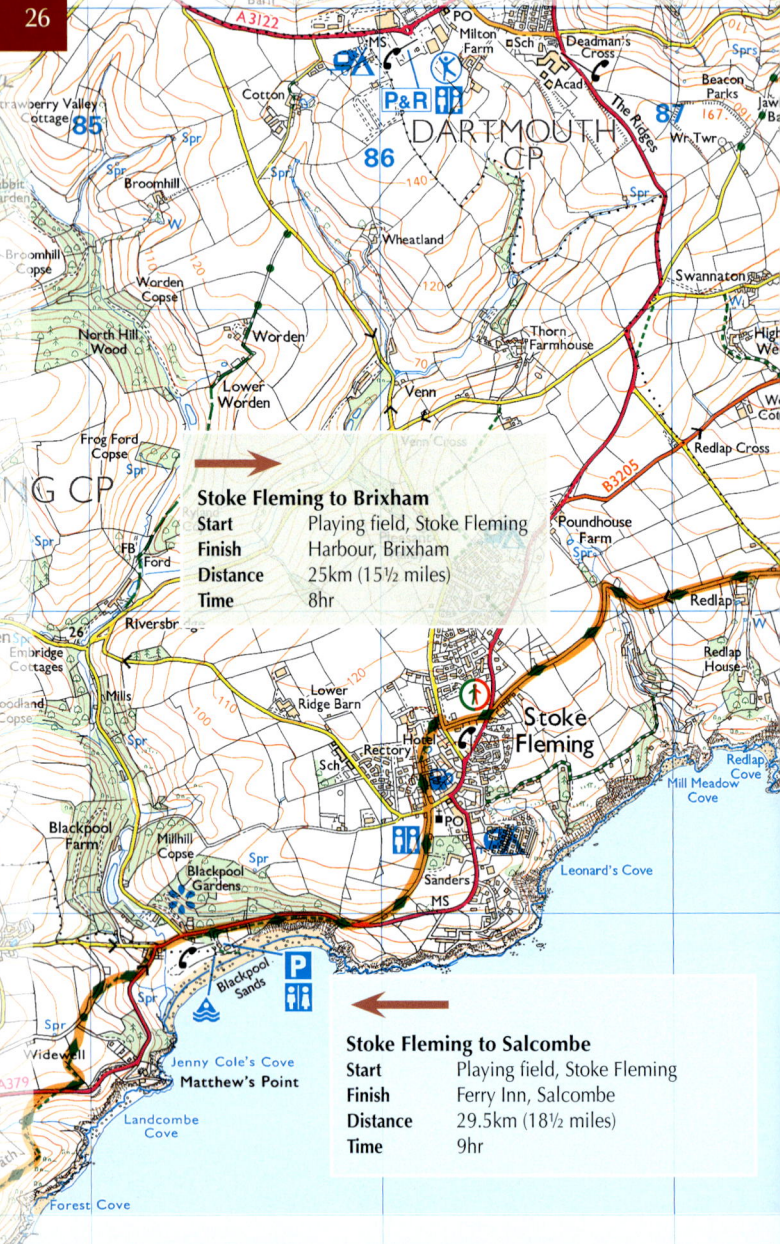

34

35

36

TEIGNMOUTH

Shaldon to Budleigh Salterton
- **Start** Ferry, Shaldon
- **Finish** Marine Parade, Budleigh Salterton
- **Distance** 22km (13¾ miles)
- **Time** 7hr

39

The Parson and Clerk
Shag Rock
East Down
Hole Head
S W C Path
Pp Ho
Caravan Park
Oakleigh Farm
Holcombe
Middle Holcombe House
Higher Holcombe Farm
Higher Holcombe House
Groynes
Breakwater
Sprey Point
Mean Low Water
Lookout Station
TEIGNMOUTH
A379

Budleigh Salterton to Shaldon

Start	Marine Parade, Budleigh Salterton
Finish	Ferry, Shaldon
Distance	22km (13¾ miles)
Time	7hr

44

45

Brandy Head
Pooliness Beach
Black Head
Coal Beach
Danger Point
South Farm
South West Coast Path
Otter Estuary Nature Reserve
Otterton Ledge
Kersbrook
BUDLEIGH SALTERTON CP
BUDLEIGH SALTERTON

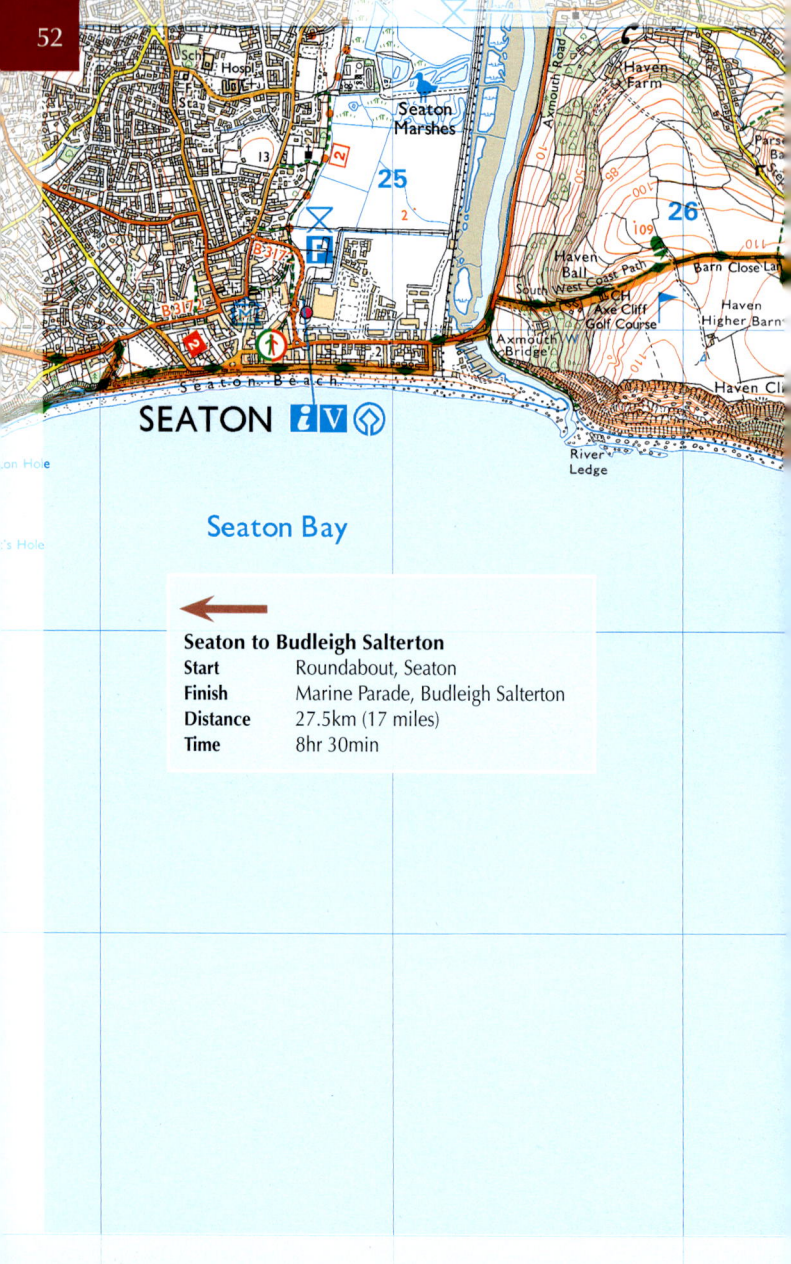

Seaton to Seatown
Start   Roundabout, Seaton
Finish   Anchor Inn, Seatown
Distance 24.5km (15¼ miles)
Time   8hr

Seatown to Abbotsbury
Start   Anchor Inn, Seatown
Finish   Grove Lane, Abbotsbury
Distance   19.5km (12 miles)
Time   6hr

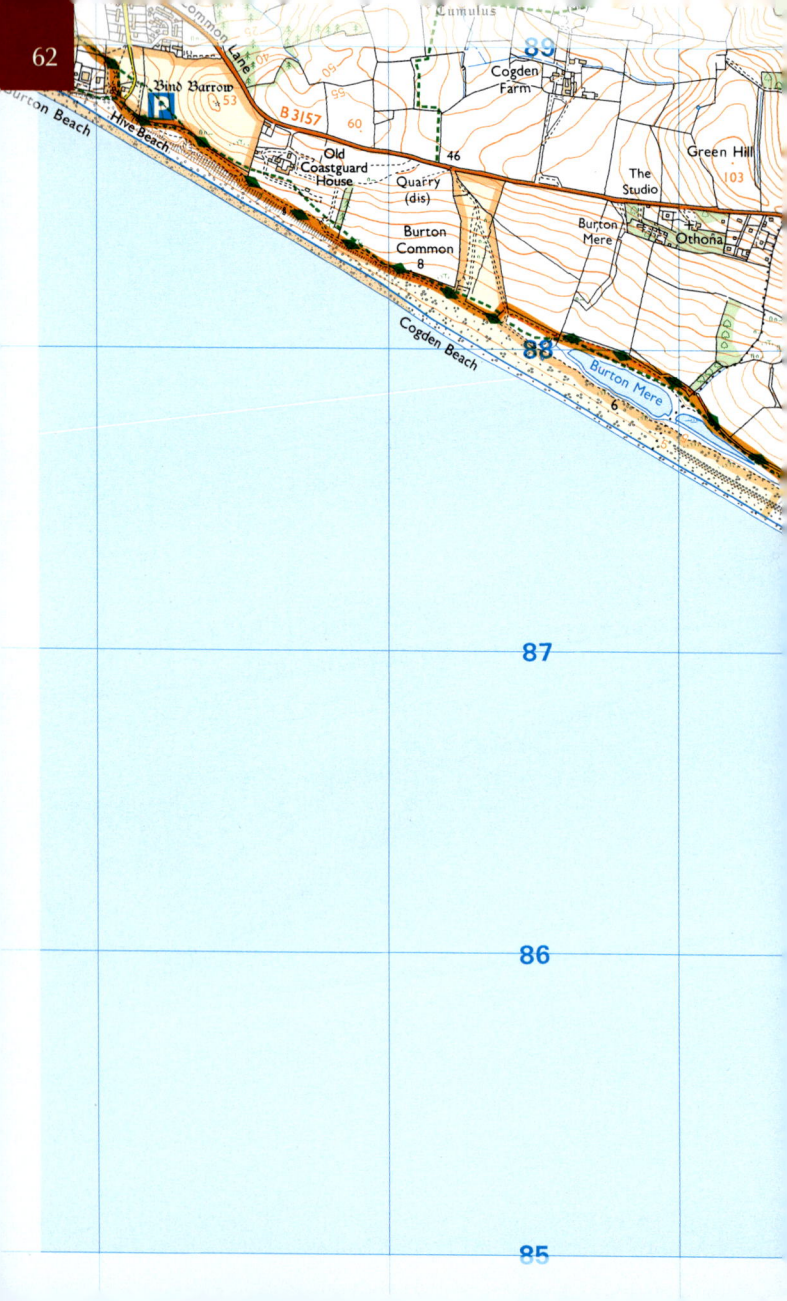

Abbotsbury to Seatown

Start	Grove Lane, Abbotsbury
Finish	Anchor Inn, Seatown
Distance	19.5km (12 miles)
Time	6hr

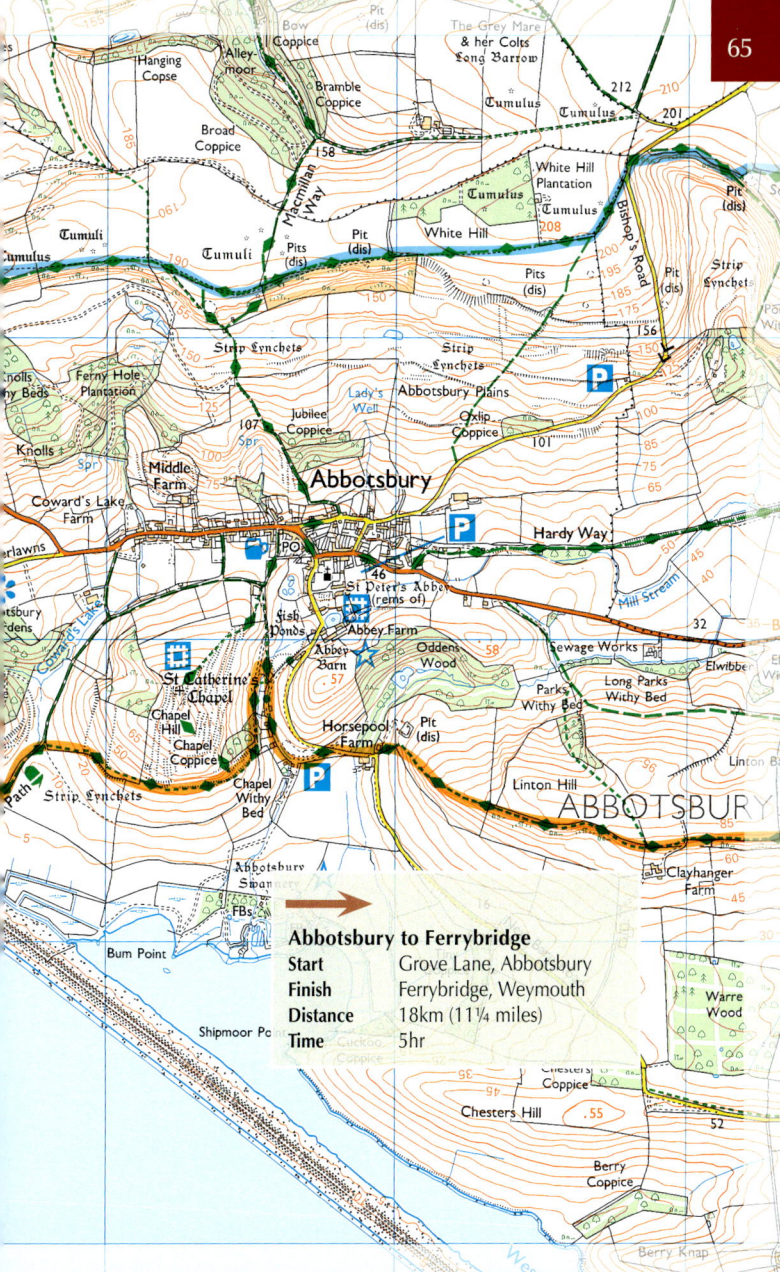

Abbotsbury to Ferrybridge
Start   Grove Lane, Abbotsbury
Finish   Ferrybridge, Weymouth
Distance 18km (11¼ miles)
Time   5hr

Ferrybridge to Abbotsbury
Start   Ferrybridge, Weymouth
Finish   Grove Lane, Abbotsbury
Distance 18km (11¼ miles)
Time   5hr

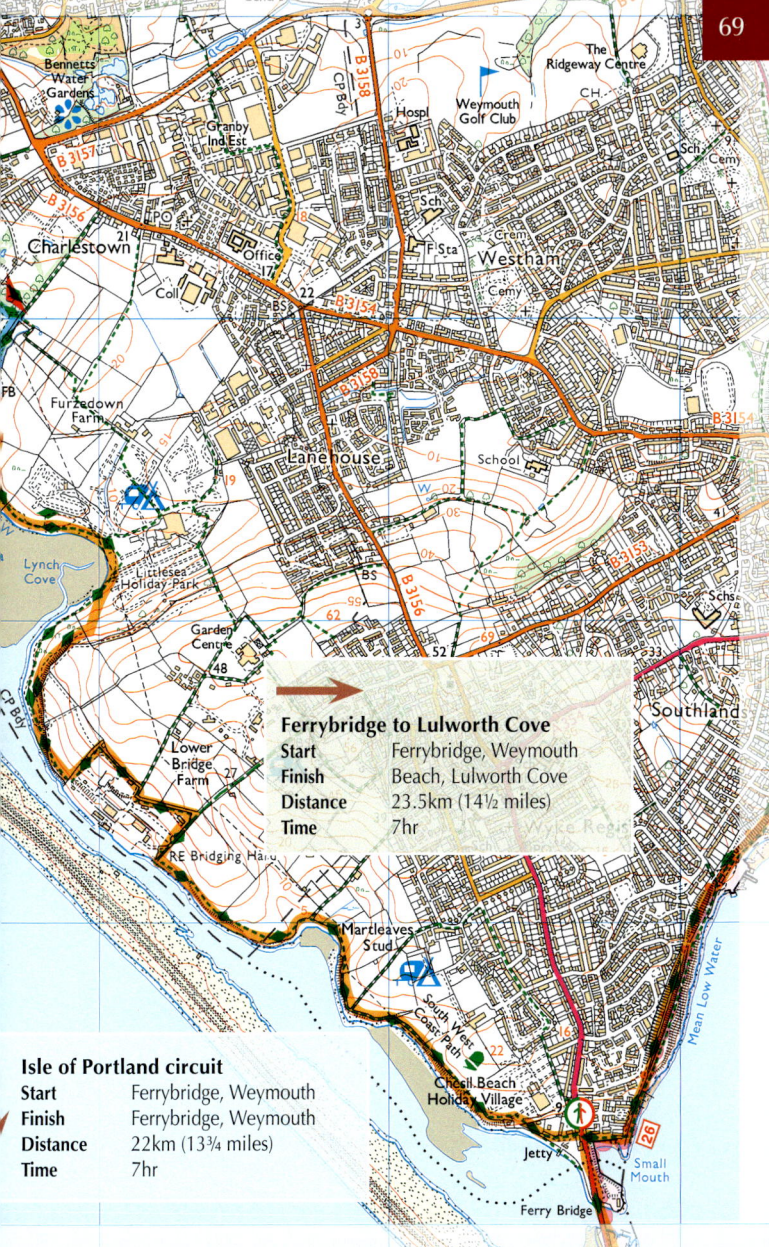

Ferrybridge to Lulworth Cove
Start: Ferrybridge, Weymouth
Finish: Beach, Lulworth Cove
Distance: 23.5km (14½ miles)
Time: 7hr

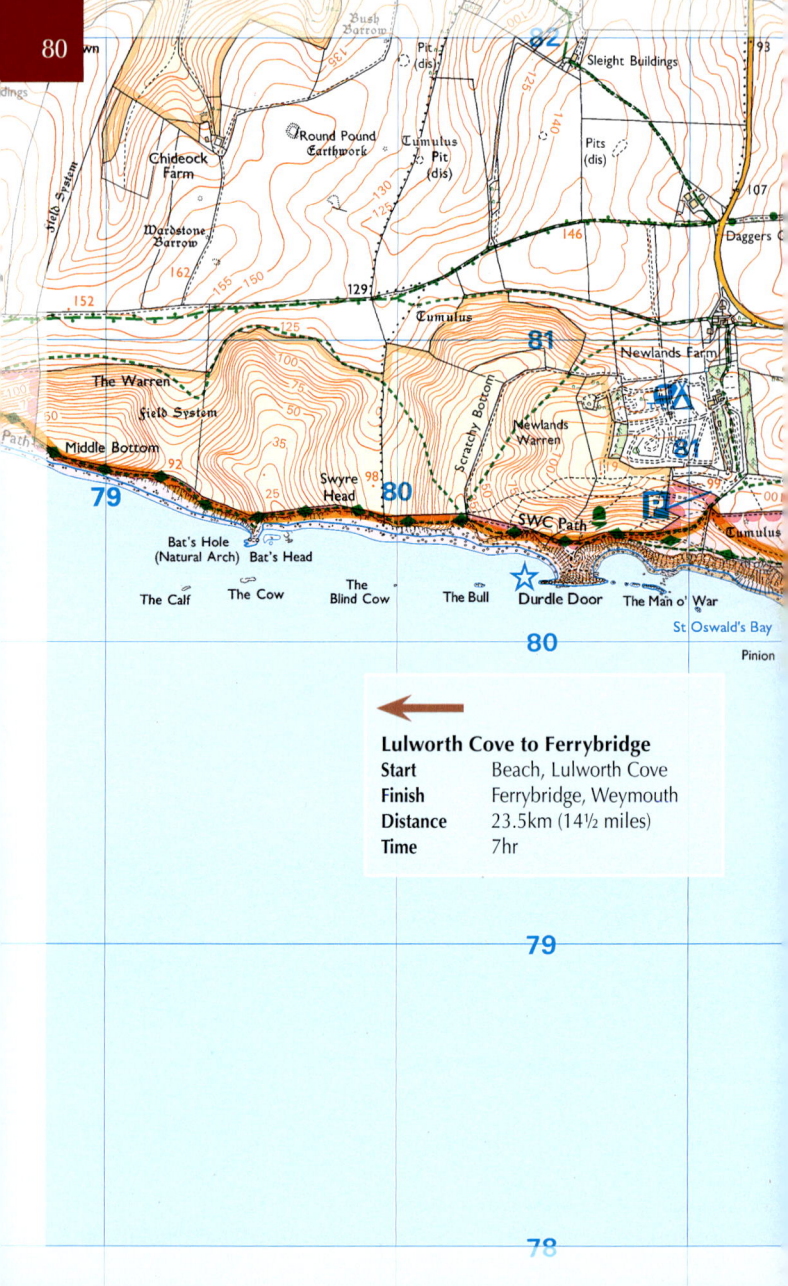

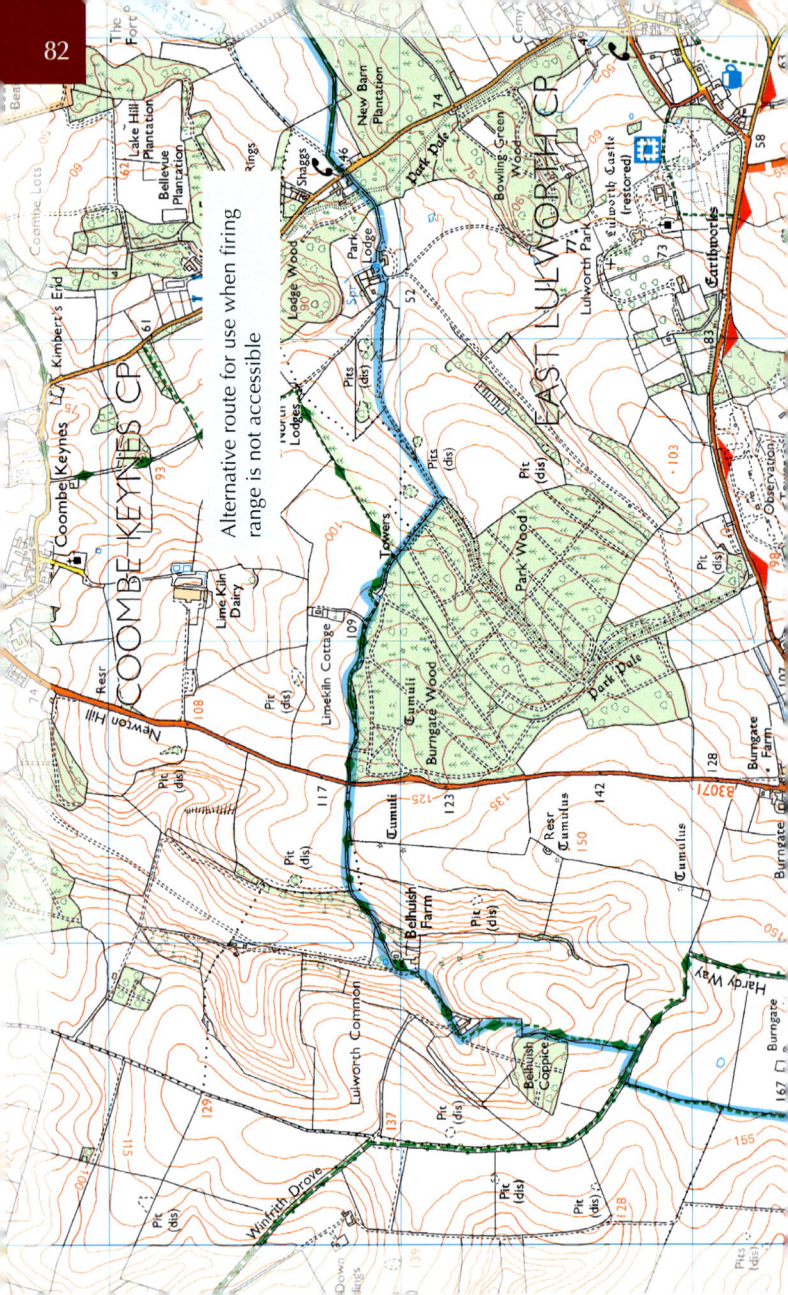

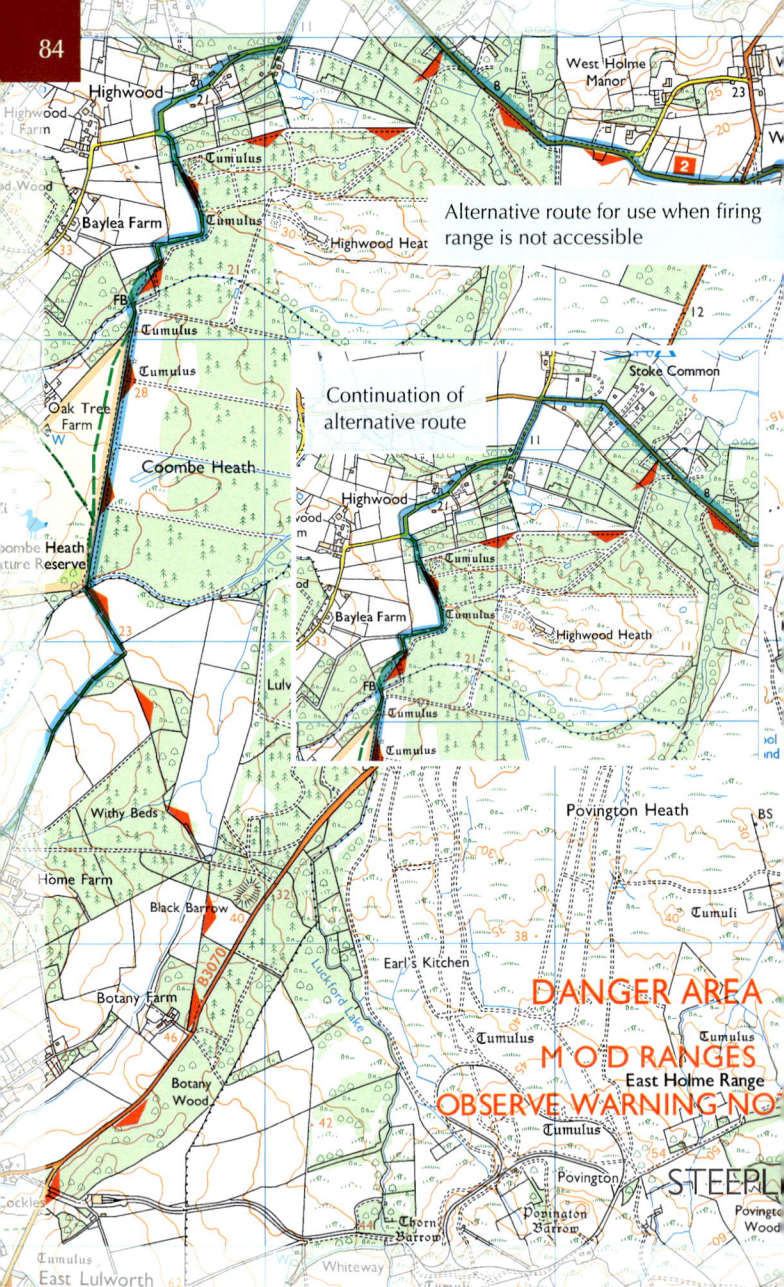

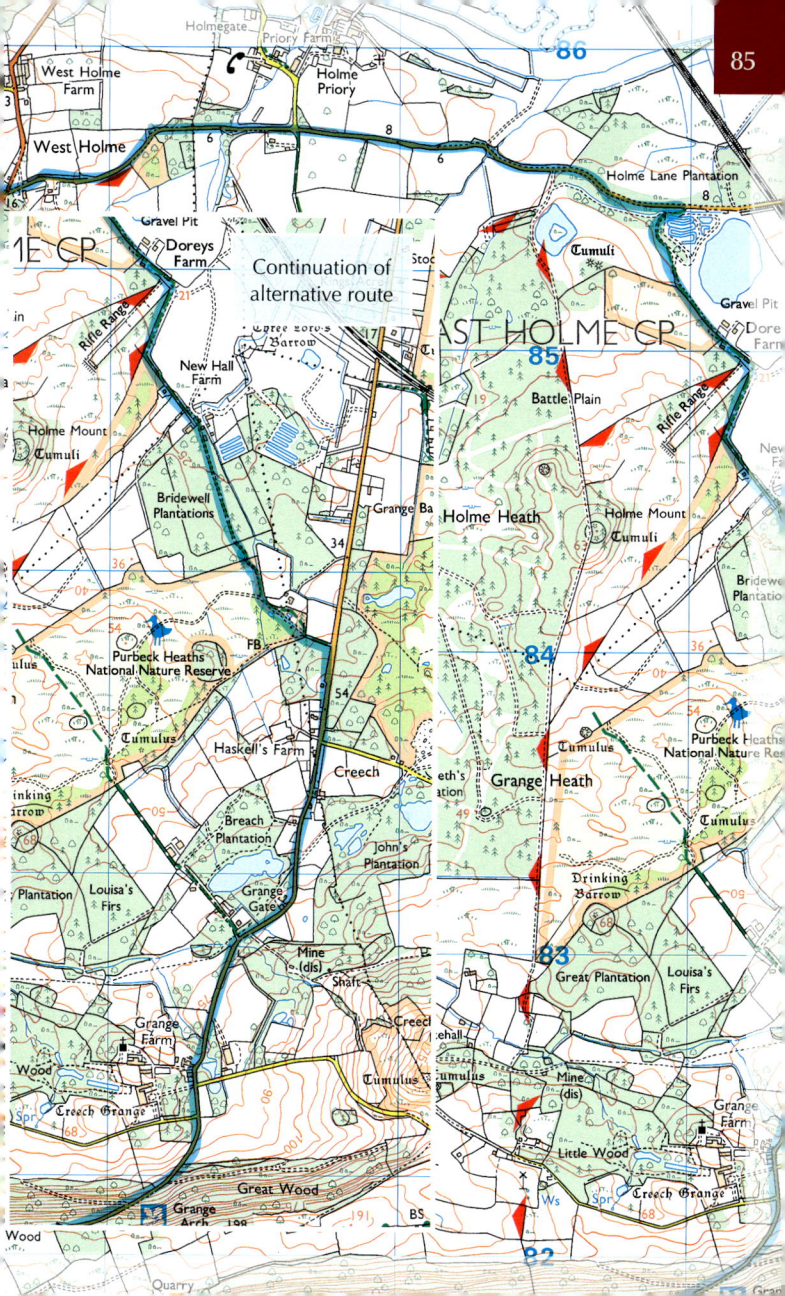

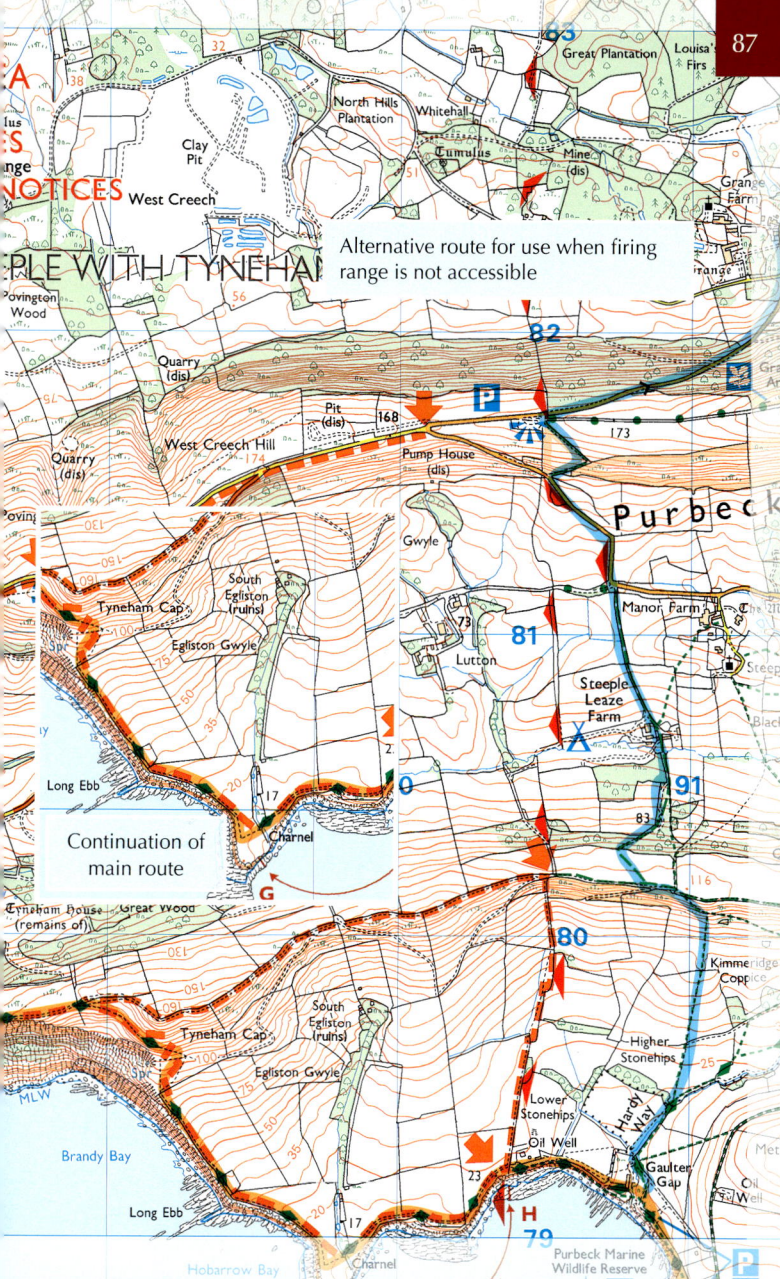

Swanage to Lulworth Cove
Start   Museum, Swanage
Finish   Beach, Lulworth Cove
Distance   33km (20½ miles)
Time   10hr

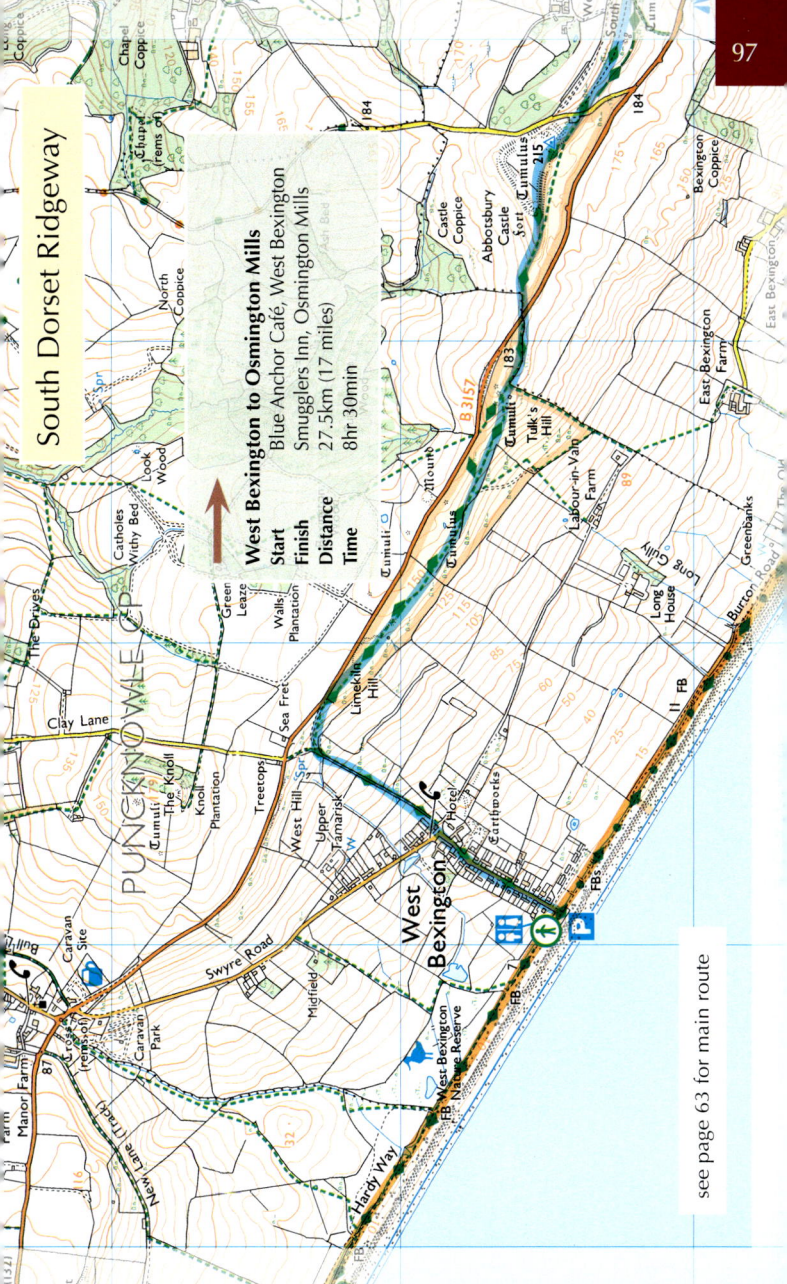

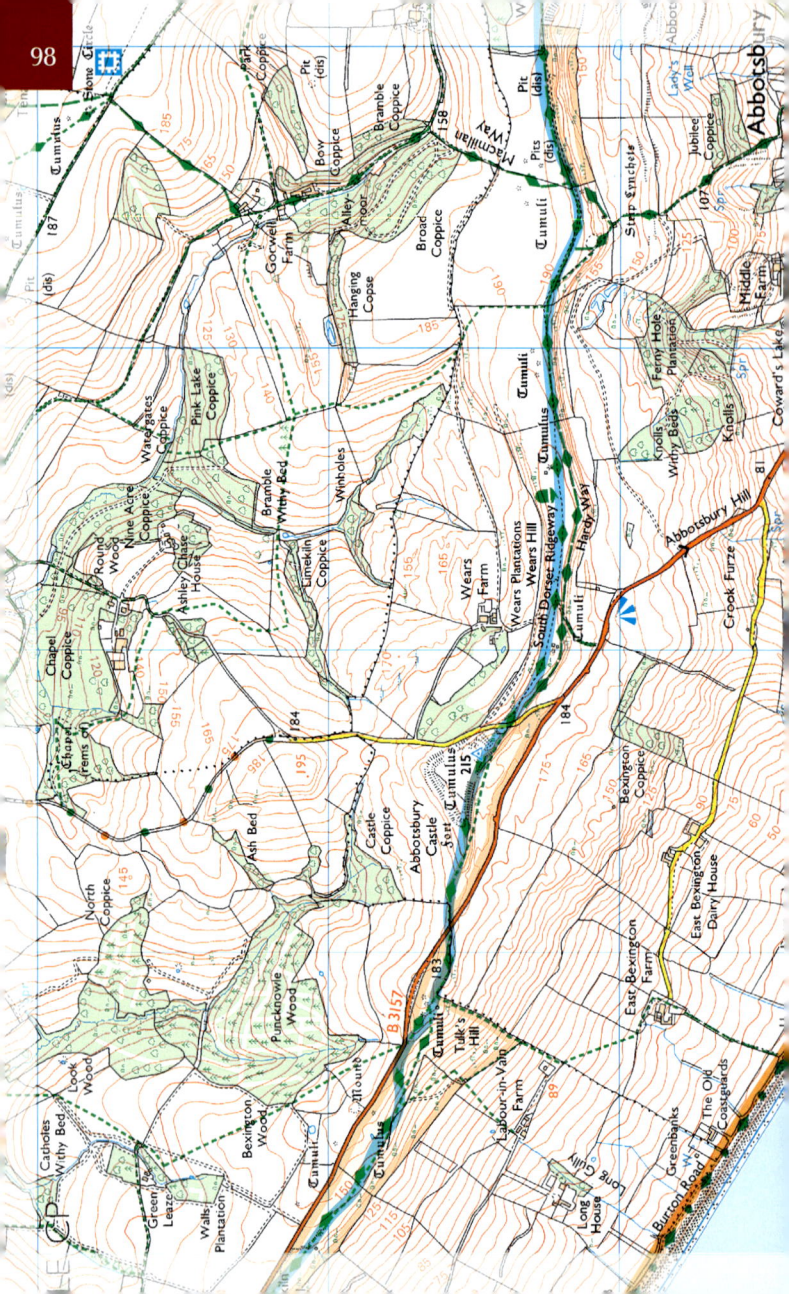

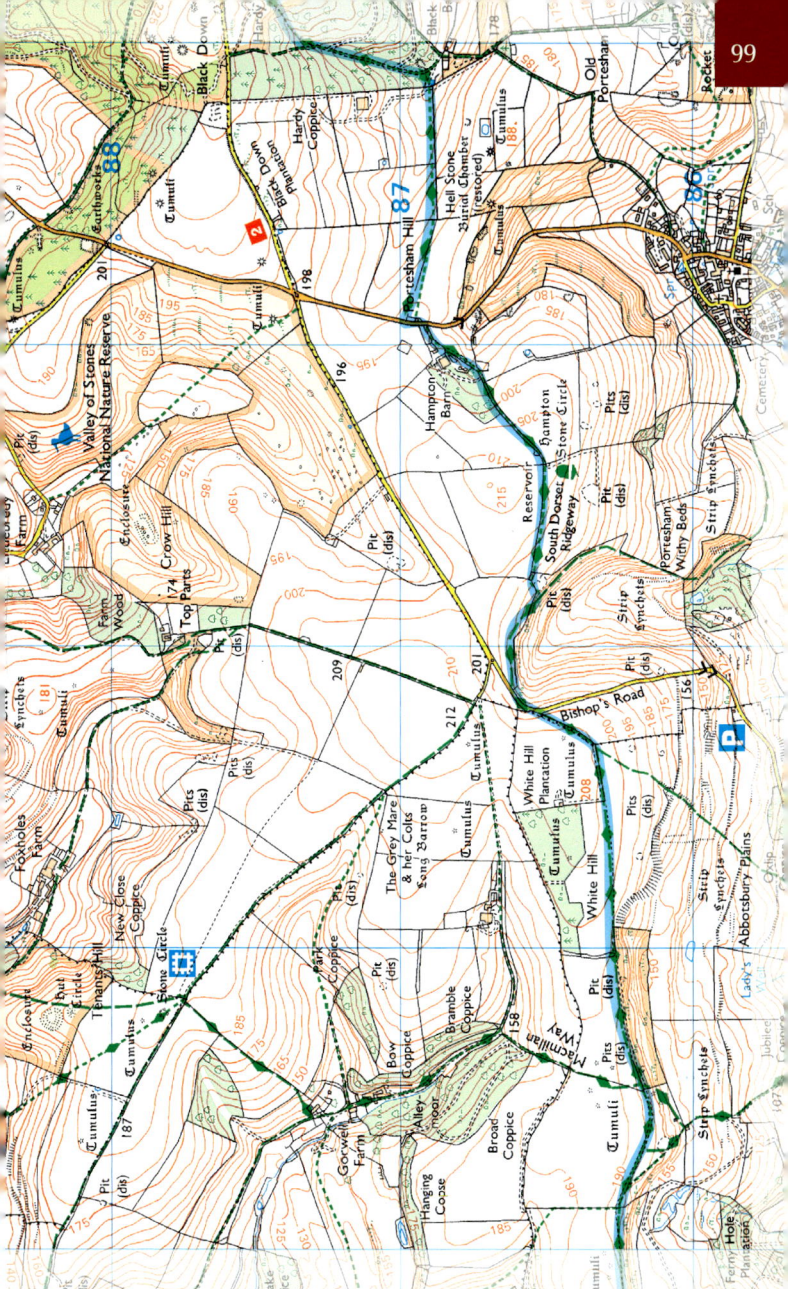

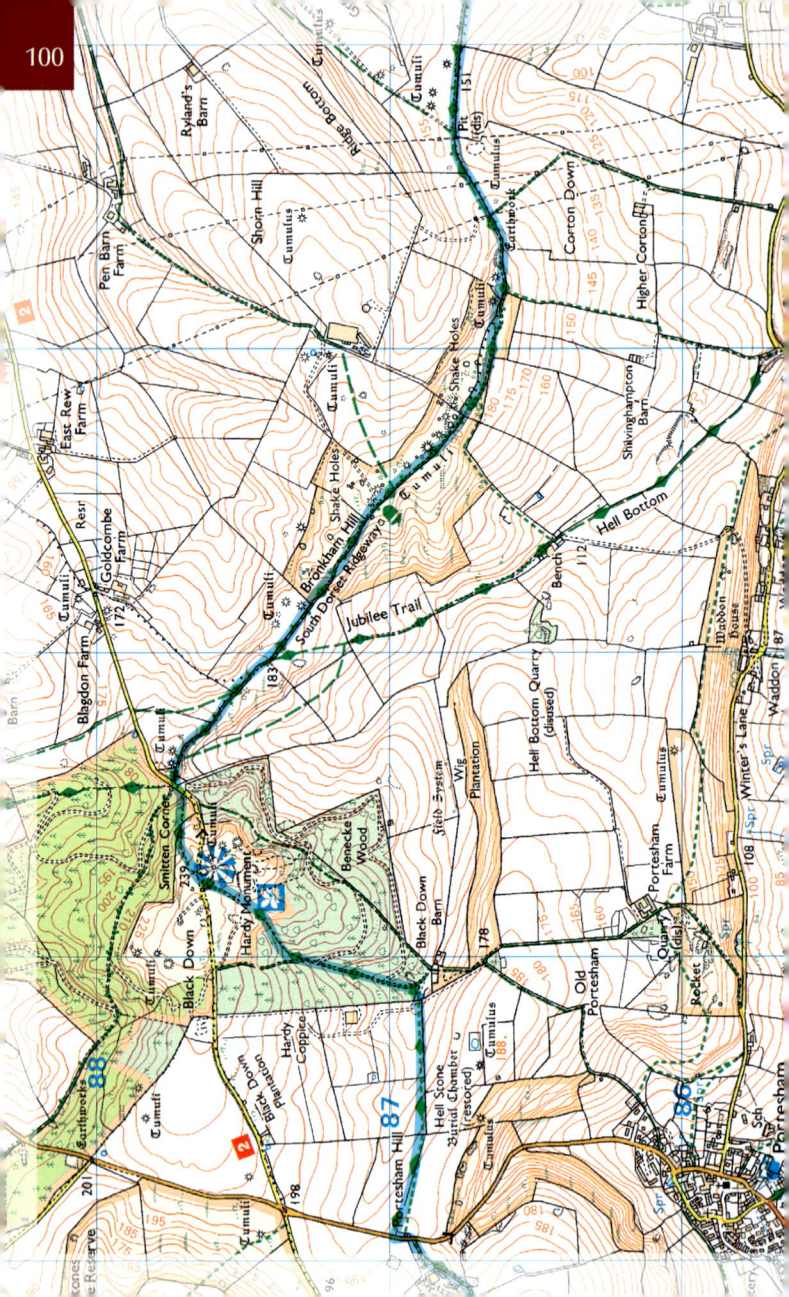

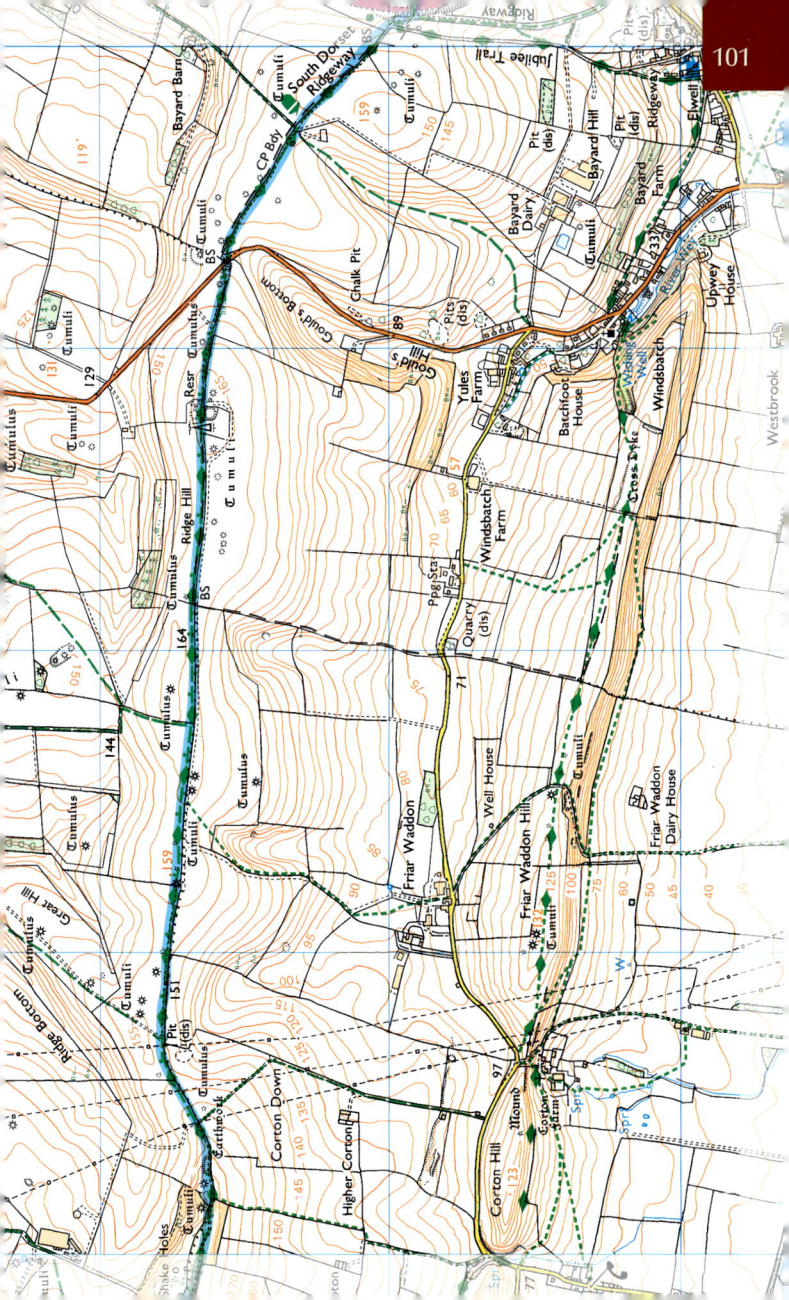

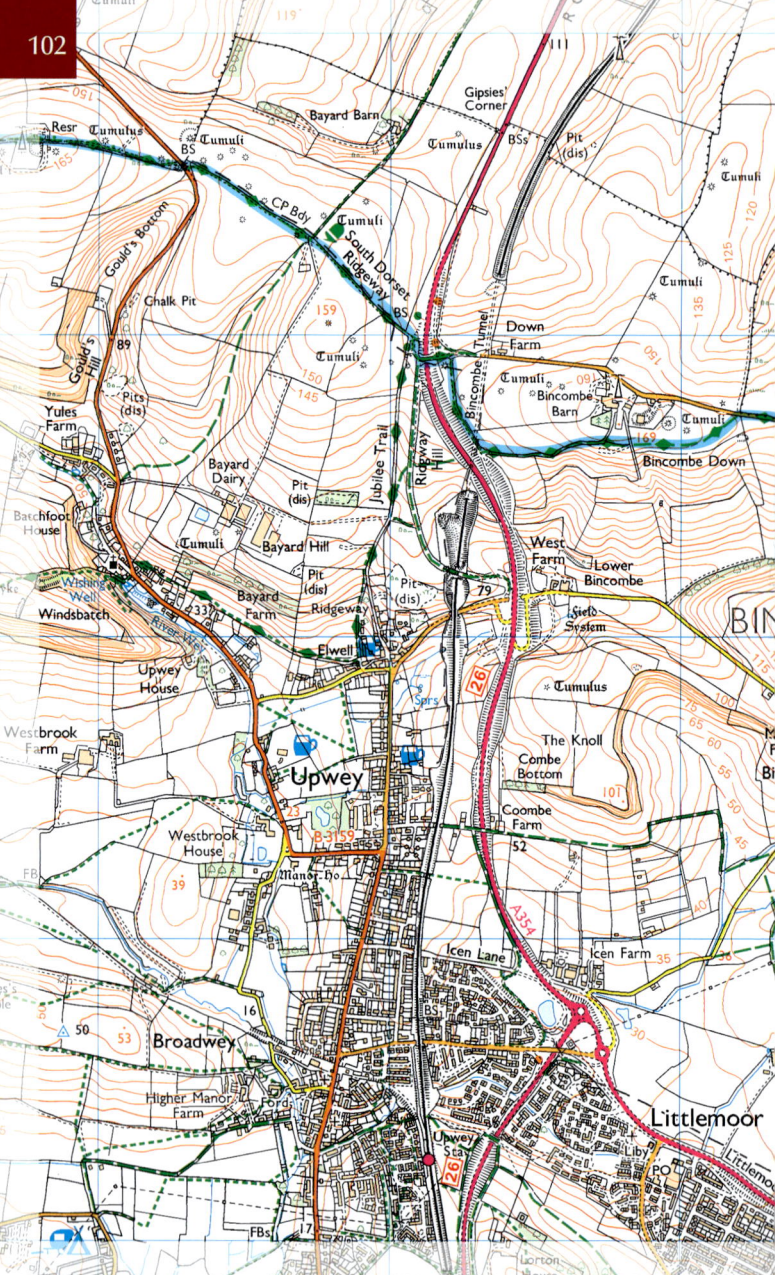

LEGEND OF SYMBOLS USED ON ORDNANCE SURVEY 1:25,000 (EXPLORER) MAPPING

ROADS AND PATHS — Not necessarily rights of way

M1 or A6(M)	Motorway
A 35	Dual carriageway
A30	Main road
B 3074	Secondary road
	Narrow road with passing places
	Road under construction
	Road generally more than 4 m wide
	Road generally less than 4 m wide
	Other road, drive or track, fenced and unfenced
>> >	Gradient: steeper than 20% (1 in 5); 14% (1 in 7) to 20% (1 in 5)
Ferry	Ferry; Ferry P – passenger only
....	Path

- Service Area (S)
- Service Area
- Junction Number (7)
- Toll road junction (T1)

RAILWAYS

- Multiple track / Single track — standard gauge
- Narrow gauge or Light rapid transit system (LRTS) and station
- Road over; road under; level crossing
- Cutting; tunnel; embankment
- Station, open to passengers; siding

PUBLIC RIGHTS OF WAY

- ---------- Footpath
- – – – – – Bridleway
- +++++ Byway open to all traffic
- -+-+-+- Restricted byway

The representation on this map of any other road, track or path is no evidence of the existence of a right of way

ARCHAEOLOGICAL AND HISTORICAL INFORMATION

⌧	Site of antiquity	VILLA Roman	✱ ⬚⬚⬚ Visible earthwork
⚔ 1066	Site of battle (with date)	𝕮𝖆𝖘𝖙𝖑𝖊 Non-Roman	

Information provided by English Heritage for England and the Royal Commissions on the Ancient and Historical Monuments for Scotland and Wales

HEIGHTS AND NATURAL FEATURES (continued)

Vertical face/cliff

Contours are at 5 or 10 metre vertical intervals

Loose rock • Boulders • Outcrop • Scree

- Water
- Mud
- Sand; sand and shingle

SELECTED TOURIST AND LEISURE INFORMATION

- Building of historic interest
- Cadw
- Heritage centre
- Camp site
- Caravan site
- Camping and caravan site
- Castle / fort
- Cathedral / Abbey
- Craft centre
- Country park
- Cycle trail
- Mountain bike trail
- Cycle hire
- English Heritage
- Fishing
- Forestry Commission Visitor centre
- Garden / arboretum
- Golf course or links
- Historic Scotland
- Information centre, all year
- Information centre, seasonal
- Horse riding
- Museum
- National Park Visitor Centre (park logo) e.g. Yorkshire Dales

- Nature reserve
- National Trust
- Other tourist feature
- Parking
- Park and ride, all year
- Park and ride, seasonal
- Picnic site
- Preserved railway
- Public Convenience
- Public house/s
- Recreation / leisure / sports centre
- Roman site (Hadrian's Wall only)
- Slipway
- Telephone, emergency
- Telephone, public
- Telephone, roadside assistance
- Theme / pleasure park
- Viewpoint
- Visitor centre
- Walks / trails
- World Heritage site / area
- Water activites
- Boat trips
- Boat hire

(For complete legend and symbols, see any OS Explorer map).

OTHER PUBLIC ACCESS

• • •	Other routes with public access	The exact nature of the rights on these routes and the existence of any restrictions may be checked with the local highway authority. Alignments are based on the best information available
♦ ♦ ♦	Recreational route	
♦ ♦ ♦ **National Trail**	**Long Distance Route**	
– – – – –	Permissive footpath	Footpaths and bridleways along which landowners have permitted public use but which are not rights of way. The agreement may be withdrawn
– – – – –	Permissive bridleway	
• • •	Traffic-free cycle route	
[1] **1**	National cycle network route number – traffic free; on road	

ACCESS LAND

 Firing and test ranges in the area. Danger! Observe warning notices

 Access permitted within managed controls, for example, local byelaws. Visit **www.access.mod.uk** for information

England and Wales

	Access land boundary and tint	Portrayal of access land on this map is intended as a guide to land which is normally available for access on foot, for example access land created under the Countryside and Rights of Way Act 2000, and land managed by the National Trust, Forestry Commission and Woodland Trust. Access for other activities may also exist. Some restrictions will apply; some land will be excluded from open access rights. The depiction of rights of access does not imply or express any warranty as to its accuracy or completeness. Observe local signs and follow the Countryside Code. Visit **www.countrysideaccess.gov.uk** for up-to-date information
	Access land in wooded area	
	Access information point	

BOUNDARIES

— + — + —	National
— · — · —	County (England)
— — — —	Unitary Authority (UA), Metropolitan District (Met Dist), London Borough (LB) or District (Scotland & Wales are solely Unitary Authorities)
· · · · · · · ·	Civil Parish (CP) (England) or Community (C) (Wales)
— —	National Park boundary

VEGETATION

Limits of vegetation are defined by positioning of symbols

♠ ♠	Coniferous trees
♣ ♣	Non-coniferous trees
	Coppice
○ ○ ○	Orchard
— — —	Scrub
⋯⋯	Bracken, heath or rough grassland
≈ ≈	Marsh, reeds or saltings

HEIGHTS AND NATURAL FEATURES

52 ·	Ground survey height	Surface heights are to the nearest metre above mean sea level. Where two heights are shown, the first height is to the base of the triangulation pillar and the second (in brackets) to the highest natural point of the hill
284 ·	Air survey height	

SOUTH WEST COAST PATH

This map booklet accompanies Paddy Dillon's guidebook to walking the South West Coast Path National Trail, from Minehead to South Haven Point. The guidebook features 1:50,000 OS mapping alongside detailed step-by-step route description and lots of planning and other information about local culture, wildlife and the protected coastline.

Inland: A gentle, winding track climbs up across steep grassy slopes from Bincombe

NOTES

NOTES

NOTES

CICERONE

Trust Cicerone to guide your next adventure, wherever it may be around the world...

Discover guides for hiking, mountain walking, backpacking, trekking, trail running, cycling and mountain biking, ski touring, climbing and scrambling in Britain, Europe and worldwide.

Connect with Cicerone online and find inspiration.

- buy books and ebooks
- articles, advice and trip reports
- podcasts and live events
- GPX files and updates
- regular newsletter

cicerone.co.uk